YOU GOTTA LET IT GO BEFORE IT TAKES YOU OVER

Poems by
Paul Koniecki, Nadia Wolnisty,
Abigail Beaudelle, Dan Provost

Kansas City   Spartan Press   Missouri

Spartan Press
Kansas City, MO
spartanpresskc@gmail.com

Copyright (c) Paul Koniecki, Nadia Wolnisty,
Abigail Beaudelle, Dan Provost 2018
First Edition 1 3 5 7 9 10 8 6 4 2
ISBN: 978-1-946642-54-7
LCCN: 2018943912

Design, edits and layout: Jason Ryberg,
Cover and title page image: unknown, but believed to have been photographed from the patio outside Frank's North Star Tavern in Lawrence, KS.
Author photos: Paul Koniecki, Roselyn Hoang, Jacob Johanson, Brian from *Zygote in My Coffee*
All rights reserved. No part of this publication may be reproduced or transmitted in any form or by any means, electronic or mechanical, including photocopying, recording or by info retrieval system, without prior written permission from the author.

Spartan Press would like to thank Prospero's Books, The Fellowship of N-finite Jest, The Prospero Institute of Disquieted P/o/e/t/i/c/s, Will Leathem, Tom Wayne, Jeanette Powers, j. d. tulloch, Jon Bidwell, Jason Preu, Mark McClane, Tony Hayden and the whole Osage Arts Community.

Paul Koniecki would like to thank the editors of *The Gasconade Review Presents: Missouri is a Ghost-Shaped Thing*, where some of these poems were previously published.

Nadia Wolnisty would like to thank these publications where some of these poems first appeared: "Fly Away Home" appeared in Winter 2018 issue of *Paper & Ink*, "How the Light Gets in" was published in a slightly different version in the anthology *Desolate Country* by EMP books, "The Pear" appeared on a menu at The Wild Detectives, Fall 2017, "The Opperation" appeared in *The University Scholar*, Fall 2011, "Epaino" appeared in the obituary section of *AZ Republic*, January 2017.

Dan Provost would like to thank these publications where some of these poems first appeared: *Red Fez, Somerville Times, Fierce Invalids-A tribute to Arthur Rimbaud, Deuce Coupe, Decomp, In Between Hangovers, The Literary Underground, The Exuberant Ashtray* and *Paraphernalia Quarterly, Chicago Record.*

CONTENTS

tuchola, my cubicle / Paul Koniecki

Belligerents / 1

Rats in Our Office / 4

Good Morning. Thank You
   For Calling _ _&_. This Is / 5

God Bless the Unknown / 8

Glorious Phantasm / 10

Hole in the Air / 11

marginal levy / 13

Caught Between Zaria and Hel / 15

Bardo / 16

Our General Manager Has an Office With a
   Rent-to-Own Fountain and a Ceiling and
   a Door / 18

Tuchola, My Cubicle / 25

Crumble (Mandatory Overtime) / 26

All Fear Is Rooted in the Fear of This Life / 27

tree's trunks are / 28

My Father Visited the Old Six / 29

disorder in / 30

anchors for candles
   gravity's wish / 31

if together is a color / 33

candles on a cake / 34

if
  when it begins to rain
  and i aspire to be / 36

on the tar-paper / 40

missing teeth falling in the rain / 41

i look over and see
   your profile in the bar light / 44

harry dean stanton says i
   can remember him anyway i want / 47

Last Night I Saw John Fante / 49

I Would Never Go Skydiving Because I Don't Want a Stranger That Close to Me / Nadia Wolisty

I'm Fucking Delicate / 53

Extra Space / 54

Protect / 60

(Little Structures) / 62

Hollow / 63

The Camera / 64

Baker / 65

Fly Away Home / 69

Poem for My Sisters / 70

The Weight of Skin / 73

How the Light Gets In / 74

Birds of Ill-Repute / 77

At Shell Station / 78

The Pear / 82

Poem for D.H. / 83

Dirt with Bits / 84

Dead Pangolin Lullaby / 85

The Operation / 87

Paradise / 91

Phenology / 96

Prayered / 97

Epaino / 99

Tapetum Lucidum / 101

The Language of Fruit Trees / Poems by Abigail Beaudelle

Hypnagogic Hymn / 105

Dream I / 106

Forest Fire — Mystery / 107

Dream II / 108

Lioness Song / 109

Dream III / 111

Helix / 112

Dream IV / 114

Basil / 115

Dream V / 116

Midwestern Woods Haiku 1-5 / 117

Interlude
   Allyson Johanson, Age 4 / 119

Dream VI / 120

Primitive / 121

Dream VII / 124

Exploit / 125
Dream VIII / 127
Fly in the Chapel / 128
Dream IX / 130
Eight is For Grief / 131
Dream X / 134
Motherhood / 135
Dream XI / 138
Mother's Day, 2017 / 139
Dream XII / 142
April Midnight / 143
Dream XIII / 146
The Kingfisher's Daughter / 147
Dream IX / 149
Monday's Broth / 150
Dream X / 153
Hypnopompic Hymn / 154

Busted Battles / Dan Provost

Old / 157
Steven Daedalus had Everything on me / 158
My Past Five Years / 160
A Thought in the Snow / 162
Righteous but Wrong / 164
World Widows / 165

Worcester State Grad Fair / 166

Reading J.D. / 167

Warren Haynes at 3 A.M. / 168

No God or Devil / 169

They Are Not Friends / 170

10 Degrees on Main South Worcester / 172

The Kings and Queens / 174

Briggs and the Shawshank Piano / 176

Depression 208 / 178

Law Abiding Citizen / 179

New York Journal Entry / 181

A Plea to Arthur Rimbaud / 182

Gutter Mind / 184

The Coffee Shop Man / 185

Willem / 187

No More Lines / 189

Finding Your Kingdom / 190

Kerouac's Fall Afternoon / 191

Looking for Johnny's Guitar String / 192

Thoughts While Walking the Dog / 194

Once a Blindness / 195

Jeff's Walk / 197

Writer's Block / 198

Tyson and Cobain / 200

Do You Care / 201

Imagery / 202

Kids in Florida / 203

Depression #122 / 204

Smoking Character / 206

tuchola, my cubicle

Poems by Paul Koniecki

Belligerents

if I die, let it be known that the Army
and I died because of this son-of-a-bitch.

-General Mikolai Boltuc speaking about
Commanding General Wladyslaw Bortnowski

Battle of Tuchola Forest 1939

For four days in September
Bortnowski refused to believe
in the existence of tanks.

Woods
death
and a refusal to retreat

this was reasonable.
Inside everything is recorded. In
life every conversation is

a conversation with yourself.
This afternoon
at work through a line of pine trees

to the east of my cubicle
out the window I heard
an ice cream truck selling my favorite
 bright orange push-ups.

Yesterday
they had us wait

in the stairwell as a tornado
touched the tops of DFW's tallest towers
this was reasonable.

Later a fifty-two year old co-worker
running back from lunch break
afraid

to be a minute late fell
and broke her shoulder
then was made

to wait four hours
crying in a seat outside the human
resources and attendance office

for permission to seek medical treatment
and not be terminated
for insubordination.

Belligerent
belligerents
belligerence

in a call-center this is reasonable.

An orange sherbet sun
setting through the clouds

shines off a bloody palm-print smeared
on a cracked bit
of parking lot cement.

The trees in a distant
Polish woods reached once
brown bark slathered

and stamped in rust-red whorls
for the far-off fading orange
butter colored light.

Rats in Our Office

Standing in our building's kitchenette
I tell Marie Curie I didn't think
the infestation of rats came from the

refrigerator, clean or otherwise, but
the ditch behind it where they execute
poorly performing representatives.

Gesturing to a geiger-counter in the folds
of her smock she signed her reply, aware
now of the proliferation of hidden listening

devices, that such is the call center life.

Good Morning. Thank You
For Calling _ _&_. This Is

Paul. Who do I have the pleasure of visiting
with today? Visiting, as if driving by a dying
friend's hospital bed with just enough time

to roll down the window and scream, the
day was not available for me to take off and comfort your
final hour. Where did they find

the recipe for script as figure of weaponized speech?
The pleasure of the call center
sentence recorded for training purposes

and sales dispute resolution at ten paces.
Then it starts and they call me, customers as
beseeching as lovers, in rapid, unending,

never ceasing, succession. Help me, give me,
help me, give, give, my wife has cancer, my husband just
died, I need a lower bill.

And during our call they think they are the desperate
ones. Life as chill process,
sentience distilled, MANDATORY VERBIAGE,

success secrets whispered by management
as cartons of milk past its expiration date
dripped into my, does this smell funny to you,

headset. *WHAT DID YOU SELL THEM ON
THAT CALL?!?* Vivid presence of the past hot
as a carousel of ghosts, distant as an

empathetic ear. How did we come to this
forest of deserts? Typing class a distant
10th grade memory. By 1 September 1939

General Heinz Guderian had more than
three hundred Panzer tanks at his disposal.
The pine and the spruce trees surrounding

my cubicle shudder in terrible flashback of
torn memory and shattered branch, my head
and my heart caught between the Brda

and the Wda Rivers a widow mad with grief
unhinging in my ear. Sliding open my desk
drawer I notice a rat has opened the

packet of soy sauce I'd saved to cheer up
lunch, I'd already given up on ketchup, off my pants leg
I see brown tears, another

sacrificed day caught in the mud at dawn.
Casualties can't be late getting back in from
lunch break, tardy, tardy, the last word

coughed as a laugh over the vermillion line
of some unclaimed body's dying, dying, lips.

God Bless the Unknown

in the microscopic space
between now
and the next ringing

call.

All we can embrace
is learning
a new thing today.

Faced with leavening,
money
withers in a pause. Authority

is the angle of incidence
of hate. Surplussed
masses,

unwashed caesura,
warranted breath
of inclusion and catch,

run, run away from
the zealots endorsing varietals
labeled, consequence, sortie, and pain.

At the Battle of Hel
the Luftwaffe bombed the
Polish peninsula into

oblivion.

Mikolaj Boltuc, an officer serving
General Władysław Bortnowski's
Pomeranian Army, regretted

in the first days of the German
Invasion, not having put
a bullet through Bortnowski's

head and assuming command.
Boltuc may have suffered
a nervous breakdown.

Wait, the next call is here.
Surveying the field below I see
a fine green

hillock pictured next to the
definitions of very and despair —
swallow deeply and answer, Hello.

Glorious Phantasm

Desperate caller on the other
end, will you dial emergency

services for me? You came on
crying, begging for assistance,

help, you are my savior, in truth
I am but another wingless,

disconnecting call.

Hole in the Air

> *It's not an easy thing to meet your maker*
> -Roy Batty

The clouds are unoccupied today
The Hubble and other telescopes
Have yet to quadrangulate a
Mansion with a security gate
In space only so many

Vacations can be granted per
Day in a call center
Job like mine archangels gods
And soldiers calling in sick
Will never do asking if

I can use a floating
Holiday to stay home today
I notice the line of
New growth pine trees aside
My cubicle wall is like

A trapping fence peering through
I see reps on calls
And Polish soldiers and German
Soldiers bleeding on the lawn
And the Battle of Tuchola
 Forest rages on and the

Telescopes still point away and
The day was not available
To take off I-Phone barking
Marching orders in terms of

Philosophy and vocabulary when the
Act of meeting the maker
Is an act of breaking
Form faith is absence and
You are your only General

marginal levy

morning break
torn hunk of warm bread

time as a race
to the next

pause
in the action

i would be a fool
to mention your lips here

torn hunk of warm bread
afternoon break

excise tax
inland duty

withholding customs
and butter

at the edges
of a borderland

soft sweet wet
i race

to the moment again when we are
able to catch and gather

mouthful of seawater
forest of blood

peninsula of hel
blown into an island

tuchola my cubicle
there are no more good

union jobs in america
your kiss your kiss

at the end of their hoary parking lot
at the end of every shift

the way salt can burn like fire
pumping blood hands flying in the air

Caught Between Zaria and Hel

I scale the impossibly
High cliffs surrounding my
Six foot by six
Foot assigned workspace pulling

Up the last three
Inches with my chin
One side forest one
Side desert one side

Ocean my eyes and
Ears go blind tongue
Save me looking down
From this star height

On the whole of
The world yelling True
Love True Love finally
The shift ends and

You are there

Bardo

As parts discombobulate to
Parting or the original
Bardo Thodol in the
West also known as

The user's guide to
Call center life and
We are trained in
The three intermediate stages

Between the beginning and
The end of a
Shift bardo of the
Moment of death bardo

Of the experiencing of
Reality and bardo of
Rebirth if the Bardo
Is a transom we

Cross steps we climb
Eternity as front porch
Beckoning and I read
The Tibetan Book of

The Dead on my
Lunch break for the
Laughs manager counting the
Seconds till I return

Our General Manager Has an Office With a Rent-to-Own Fountain and a Ceiling and a Door

(Dream in direct deposit and tangerine)

Red gelding in a pop-up
Cheap and dirty origami box
Chair in my cubicle
War Horse you are a motte

And a broken mineshaft with
A barely working height
Lever and I keep the seat
As close as I can to the floor

Each tour is the cruel life-cycle
Of an impacted wisdom tooth
Guised as a tender cutlet
Corroded horse I smell lilacs in the

Childhood home my mother loved
Or beaten chair of ichor and salt
More likely I am hoarfrost
And you are the buck

Everyday I approach this
Maiming field in banknote green
And I am terrified
Chair of misappropriation I love-hate

Chair Arms my nails have dug into
Throne of nothingness and tunnels
To the bottom of the hour
Best friend

A circle is a promise
A promise is a hole
A tube in a circle is three
Snakes eating you

The office rats and opossums run away
At eight a.m. I hear the order
Given to advance
Hungry tired huddled caviar

Cut crystal cave-art
Or burglars hanging frameless
On the far wall
Cross stitch nailed up behind

A three teak tree
General Manager's desk that reads
Tax exempt churches explain
why Heaven has a coverage charge

Headless Voice in
The empty headset in
My cubicle on my
Desk bellowing repeatedly

Whatever the plan
If you are here
It went wrong
Again and again

My manager's manager
We call The American Spring
PTSD Tattoo
Second Line

The Last General
And as well
The General's General who
Has never sung along

To Townes Van Zandt's,
If I Needed You, instead
If any noise above
The tortured's screams nothing

But pop bubbling in
Streams of clotted cream
And rancid port where
A spill becomes a stain

An injury an injury a
Bench warrant or more pain
Back at my desk
Ear full of someone

Else's story, the Battle
Of Tuchola playing out
My window on repeat
Scratched lottery ticket

Asking have we lost again
While all I'm able to mutter
To quell my customer's pain is
A poem to my true love like this

I need the best flowers
I need the best flowers
Five dollars can buy today
As I am only flush

Just now in minutes
Blood and luck and
My love deserves to
Read every single day

How the cut of
Her hips can make
A diamond blush
Off of one of

Those fancy little cards
Tucked between the
Petals and the thorns
Sensing my desperation the

Voice on the other
End tries to comfort
Me as my manager
Sends me a message

Popping on my ragged
Screen reading *close and
See me after this call*
Tepid cup of water my only defense

And the phone rings
Day-Job gray again and they are poor
Whatever the plan if you are here
It went wrong

Honey wine figs tax exempt gods death
Comes at the welcome affordable end
The old forest in Poland
Begins to pray and fight again

Today the hold button
On my computer telephone
System is broken consequently
The crying never stops

My pc's mouse is
A spider or an intrauterine device
When I die I know the sound
Of rats chewing through wires

And brimstone and fire
Will be the sound
Of an incoming call
The eyelashes on my

Coworker's faces are frozen red
I cannot blow them away and wish
Them to their rewards
Long escape by gentle

Falling gravity requires a greatly
Elevated starting point
On lunch break in an ancient
Polish woods on the forest floor

I find a poem titled *Shoulda*
Which reads as follows
Driving to the thrift store yesterday
I found an old and long forgotten

Poem written on the
Back of a to-go menu
Dated SPECIALS Aug 8, 2017
Passing it along after

So many years may
Be a mistake and people will say
That I was too young
And that it

Was poorly written
But if they knew you then
They would never say
That I was wrong

And the bullets and
The screaming manager's
Screaming dollar signs spewed
As a rented geyser spews anon

I imagine later
Greeting my love with poetry
Dripping from my lips
A desert flower opening at

The first hint of rain
The top-knot of the coworker
In the stall next to me
Lands on my desk

Marie Curie and Wislawa
Szymborska scream and wipe
The wayward fore-skull takes the fifth
Continuing as usual the killings go on

Tuchola, My Cubicle

Phantasm, a row of spruce appeared
to the left of my desk this morning
just before eight. My shifts begin

precisely as ordered.
This morning, after the trees, Marie
Sklodowska Curie sat beside me

to plug in and listen to my calls. I
said, my name is Moreski.
Handing back my 'do not resuscitate

papers' and wiping my headgear Curie
noted how my chair croaked at the broken places,
my morning scabbard shined,

my workstation thrummed. She felt
the terrible sound of an imminent attack.
Shaking, her lunch orange rolled onto

the floor over the masking tape line
in the carpet that marks the place
I do not have a door.

Crumble (Mandatory Overtime)

The hours are disembodied legs
walking nowhere and the word
'extinction' scratched into a placard

below a mostly broken statue seemingly
not of this celestial body but an empty piece
of sky serving you a court order written

in a language you will never speak. Tender
moments your eyes are basalt and fire.
When morning comes I break in two

places and realize all knowledge begins
with imagination and words actively fighting
to not become another victim of their own

experience. Even paintings want to be
recognized and seen. We land at night
on the surface of the lake next to a picture

of the moon.

(ring, ring, ring.)

All Fear Is Rooted in the Fear of This Life

The walls even walk in drab clothing.
Fluid, the corridors compress
and retract. Timpanis idle in reverse

pressing on an unclean ear. Day one
I hold a gold clutch and an orange
headband in my hair as they hang

a security badge on a lanyard about
my slag-bump shoulders and down
my beating neck. Worse than silent

a throat wails. Waiting to use the
microwave or the commode, delicately,
I touch the tattoo on the neck in front

of me. A thousand years pass. The
plate in the oven spins. The water spins.
An alarm screams me back to the desk.

tree's trunks are

bent legs dancing
discarded socks and

shoes scattered flowers
on the lawn

i wish the
job would cover

their brilliant window
glass with blinds

or drapes i
am a lost

bird fear of
freedom is real

life rolling on
out there beyond

the desk short
legs long turning

in the sun

My Father Visited the Old Six

story office building where I work.
We went to the roof for

the view. A bunting mistook a
window beneath us for air. Stunned

but unharmed it flew off. Unlike
some apartments in China the old

six dons no net to catch
her jumpers. At night I struggle

to breathe through their ragged mouths.
A pair of famulus make a

single congeries. Being the last union
job we had orders to leap

to our deaths. Science extended its
arms to catch a pair of

compass roses. Falling more slowly
than snow the sky ran. We hugged.

We leapt. We flew. Stunned but
unharmed the war ended. Thank gravity.

disorder in

if i place
another letter here

sentence a phrase
to life

or sky with hands
when rocks

at other sites of worship
formed a circle

a conjuration of delirium
a reverie

eternizing in a dream
your secret given name

anchors for candles
gravity's wish

how do you
write down
blowing out a flame

i'll climb
your bones
and move slowly

long brush
in a short
jar

radio tower
in a cloud
you —

descending
arms   out
and angled

straight as a fence
you —
rabbit of the no snares

all the deities
nose-pressed to the glass
the moon is also

two heads
all four of our eyes
are spun closed

skull on skull
wondering if
we will ante up again

heaven is
a book
your sockets

are paintings
only more articulate
i am

the earth in love
you fly into
a paragraph

stave cantos woman
the world is
a riot of ink

in the
leaves
of your hand

if together is a color

and form
a wild thing dying in the night

you whisper origin stories
the provenance to fashion

to devise
to work from home

to screw down on reality
and me

formless hard and flourishing
the city's lights are flowers

ive planted in your name
petals minutes run

across an ecstatic skyline
previewing the foreplay

of the wind
and what is left when we rage against the light

candles on a cake

it's plain to see the moon
is in my eyes tonight instead

wind is defined as what is left
of yesterday

we are where forever goes
silver over gold

i close my eyes to call down
a book of jubilee

an arc of trampolines and
circuitry burning across the sky

a thousand titles and lines
i have yet to write bring me

to a picture of your face
they say the wind made me crazy

i blow out more and more to start
a thousand fires and bright

and lightless nights again
circles within circles circling

we are where it ends
little deaths spooning in a pile

pigeons over bread
love

terminus indigenous
they say the wind made me crazy for you

if
when it begins to rain
and i aspire to be

the answer
to our

imaginary

children's harried question

where
is the umbrella

like
beachheads catching running dogs
like cats desiring

attention

like surf-spray
like raindrops
like sand
like sun

like happy tear-ducts
like imagination
green

or appearing to be
green
jade
emerald
lime and/or chartreuse
siberian tigers running amok from
hartford or newark or mars

in a kind way
to play or romp in play
pretending as

thundering herds
of terra-cotta wildebeests pretend

playing out scenes from madeline
l'engel's a wrinkle in time

in the kitchen
and the den
the vestibule
the veranda
the aviary
and the waiting room

if we had a den and an aviary and a
waiting room
between the veranda and the vestibule
we don't have

music swelling foreshadow and backstory
on the rise

cut-out tornadoes
life

hail and hardship and emergency broadcast
sirens be damned

over all of this sound

din and neighbors'
dins speech as
espionage
mental warfare
stripped wallpaper or checks
pulchritude
or excessive homeliness set aside

and the uselessness of useless noise
dying to be heard

for if you'll consider for a moment every
sound you've ever heard is a dying sound's
last gasp

before this and everything and you
i drop to my knees

praying to all things that exist or
don't in this dimension or less
folding and unfolding like my

grandfather's
accordion

as i try to be and be for many reasons
of ego and science
existence and love

your answer to any and all
umbrella queries
philosophical tertiary or otherwise

the shortest flight feathers
nearest the body
on the rear edge of a bird's wing

in the rain

on the tar-paper

roof

you called your
garden i held

your melting heart like
the blue sky and
the white clouds

dancing chrysanthemum
morifolium in the corner
weeping broken petals

stubbed-out cigarettes
and stolen beer

missing teeth falling in the rain
-for Chin the Mango Juice

i melt
like some forgotten cup
balancing hot-cold and alone
on a shrinking patch of shade
behind the drug store

under a parapet of brick
holding the thesaurus i use as a pillow
or a note from friends
are you listening
it was a time of soiled bedrolls

and empty parking space
lemon-yellow lines and dreams of falling
showering in a hand sink
four-feet off the floor
praying for an allowance

of common soap and uncommon privacy
the sound of movement in the morning
steering wheels — tires humming
sour bodies and sweet gasoline
pulling in on itself like urban origami

Chin the Mango Juice remembers rest
in the common verity of repose
like an absent limb finding a missing itch
dry heart — dry eye — dry well
i have not the words for this

the assistant drug store manager
in her garden takes notice and approaches
to shake me off the small comfort
of a wee dark spot oozing need
like molasses

why are you lying down
i bring her to me
the blacktop is hot and glassy
on my back
pulling against the buttercup growing

in my chest
our breath goes up and down
opening and closing the ground
like a lid and the rising heat
saturates the spirit so foreign

and close
i hear love-songs / mad-songs to
the apparitions and the heat
i have burned dead grass for body hair
teeth are clouds and the wind

blowing through them hurts
i like stacks of ripping things
dirty wings
missing teeth
lap-dance for me

sweat is a wound and an ocean of rank
i am sweat
i am my life — a wreck erected
behind the diamond shamrock
i am in league with dripping things

chalk dust cops — erasers cleaned
cotton mouth — liquor store
wine in the forest — forest in the door
sun in a ditch off the edge
of a dick-dead shadeless parking lot

the color of a gun
pink like love and my dry tongue
the taste of hats and drums
and cigarettes and the left
side of my cheek

from the kisk of scissors
to the nailing lid
lick the empty buttercup
and hold something
like the sun

i look over and see
your profile in the bar light

elbows akimbo
hips and lips

catching the redness
from the curtains

and the color bulbs
in this night club

three-hundred
and ninety-eight degrees

is more than one full circle
catching

the speed-wobbles
without a skateboard

or a hill
while focusing

back on your lips
you mention the word foci

being being the plural of focus
and i pass it on

to both my eyes
and sets of images in

double vision
the bartender i texted

some poems
about her poems kisses

me over the bar
and it tastes like carmex and cigarettes

she has a shoulder tattoo of saturn
i pull away looking for your lips

and am sucked
out the door into the night

outside the dallas skyline is a
kaleidoscope

of light in a basket
falling down a lightless well

the universe loves you and
i offer to make you my favorite

banana honey and peanut
butter sandwich

with a side order of dawn
the ground reclaims the fallen

someone enters your circle for
a reason

she hands me two pieces
of toast

two minutes two hours two
days of perfection

reunion tower glitters
the parking lot opens up and
swallows me whol

harry dean stanton says i
can remember him anyway i want

my maternal grandfather's
given name was jerome

but everyone called him harry
grandma ann sang i want that man

i cant answer for the dean part or
anything beyond my own bad choices

but if you knew ann then you'd have
seen he never stood a chance

it's an understatement
to say that i am jealous

of the painters and the actors
and the sculptors self-evidently

covered in each day's miraculum
knowing i'd give anything

for a studio of my own
to have something to come out from

i even put on a bowler
and an eye patch before

i sat down just now only to find
nothing helps this poem

Last Night I Saw John Fante

before the end in a dream,
his not mine.

Or Josh Weir.

A healthy younger man explaining
the gravity of whiskey

and reading Delmore Schwartz
flat as a broom

on the floor
having missed the chance

to catch something
as solid as the wall.

Last week he called me
from a public pool in

Midland, Texas surrounded
by splashing children

shouting I'll get you little
heathens and a poem

he had just written
for the Princess of Bunker

Hill or South America. We
laughed at Facebook

phone
reception and I read him
my latest poem too. The

air crackled
drunk with words and love

I Would Never Go Skydiving Because I Don't Want a Stranger That Close to Me

Poems by Nadia Wolnisty

I'm Fucking Delicate

I'm fucking delicate, like a box of tacks.
I have my own small ceremonies
and precautions for gathering myself
into corners and out from underfoot.

When the flood comes, which it will,
I will rise to the surface, when sturdier stuff
like nails and love will sink.

I can see it already—my home
in six feet of water from the creek.
The trunk full of books and board games,
the built-in cupboards, and fireplace
inoperable and rooted down below.

I'm not sure you could call it a tack
at that point, slimy and affixable to nothing.
A plastic bulb moving too quickly to stab.
But there, stubborn and barely noticeable—
See, I unname even myself.

Extra Space

Along Clark Road in Duncanville, Texas
is a sign that reads *Extra Space Storage.*
It's across a squat, single-story, cement building with
garage doors.
The letters on *Extra Space Storage* are sort of bubbly,
like the kind you made in middle school,
along with that cool S.
The bottom half of each letter is green,
and the top half is purple.

It's a ghastly color combination
on an otherwise prosaic building.
The roof of the building is orange,
and the whole thing looks like a paradox,
which is doubly upsetting, because a paradox
is not a thing something should look like.

I think most people know what is meant.
It's a place where folks can put their extra junk
they've accumulated or inherited
and feel secure about it without having to look at it.
Pool-tables and trunks and kayaks go there.

I have nothing that fancy,
but I do have closets full of clothes that I've gotten too
large for, but can't abandon, just in case I lose
that weight again.

Just pay the fee every month,
and we're all set to ignore history.
Storage unit.
A way of letting go without
actually having to let go.

But I like to imagine that *Extra Space Storage* means
something else.
That it means extra space.
That it's a storage place for all that extra space you've
accumulated or inherited.
That space he leaves when he won't sleep in your bed
anymore and the covers seem so loose.
That space in your gut when you get leave a message
at the tone.
That space when plans get canceled or postponed
indefinitely.

Because maybe, just maybe, there's some sort of device,
like a giant ice-cream scooper,
we can use to scoop up that emptiness from all aspects
of our lives
and put it in garbage bags
and drive to Duncanville, Texas
and put it in a garage.
It's ridiculous, and I realize this.
Perhaps it's not what you might call healthy,
but I think about it every time I drive by
on my way home from work.

The lights are on at all hours,
and that's comforting in a way,
to know where that extra space storage is,
especially if you're drunk and driving home after midnight.

I guess what I'm getting at is I want to believe
that places like *Extra Space Storage* exist
because I have no idea what to do with loneliness.

Other aspects of my life I've managed to sort of channel
into something productive.
Angry about a social issue? Go to a protest meeting.
Have incredible self-destructive tendencies?
Speak out about them.
Have a difficult past? Do a TED talk and become
inspiration porn.
And blah blah, blah blah.

But loneliness is a tough one.
There's obvious things to avoid,
like random hook-ups or excessive masturbation.
Check and … check.
Not feeling sorry for yourself. Check,
expect for that one time I was naked and puking
all over myself,
because my cat had thrown-up, which lead to me puking,
which led to me puking again,
and because my vomit was making me puke,

I took off my pajamas and
threw up all over everything,
including my copy of *Brothers Karamazov* and that
yellow dress that really was too tight anyways,
but I think those kind of exceptions for not feeling sorry
for yourself are okay.

But there's more subtle ways that loneliness
can become a sort of black hole that sucks everyone
and everything into it.
We've all met people like that. Texts that say *Hey.*
Awkward, inappropriate complaints.
Timothy and Michael and Trevor and Lena from college
were like that.
Nice enough people, but they would guilt
everyone into hanging out with them.
Sometimes, they'd bribe with beers and compliments.

The whole thing was itchy,
and you told yourself you were a martyr
or that you don't know how to have appropriate
boundaries.
There's a lot of Sad, Lonely things a person can do,
and I want to know how to avoid them all.

And that's not enough, I think.
You can't just avoid doing those Sad, Lonely things;
you actually have to do something meaningful
with those feelings of isolation.
And I have no idea what that looks like.

I was having a shitty day once,
and I seriously considered asking random people
on the street what they do with loneliness.
Maybe they would be happy to have someone to talk to.
Maybe we could learn something from each other.
But then I realized that that was an incredibly Sad,
Lonely thing to do,
so I looked for that fried chicken place I heard about and
had lunch instead.

I don't see anyone in the parking lot ever
at *Extra Space Storage,*
making or not making connections with each other.
No one comes to drop off or to collect.
There's certainly never any television crews out there,
even though it's my understanding shows are built
around this sort of thing.

I wonder about the attendant—
in both the real and the imaginary versions.
In the real version, is there an attendant all of the time?
I mean, there can't be that much to do.
But maybe he has to be there,
day in and day out.
Maybe it's in the contract.
Maybe folks would just feel better knowing someone
were on location
with their kayaks and pool-table and other things
they've tried to love.

In the imaginary version, the *Extra Space Storage,* version,
he's not an attendant; he's a guard.
He has a solemn duty.
He does it with great dignity and care.
He sets the thermostat in the winter, the AC in the summer.
He watches everyone's extra space, makes sure it doesn't get
too big.

And I'll talk to him at great length, some day.
I'll work up the courage and find a way
that talking to strangers won't be a Sad, Lonely thing to do.
I'll ask him about his day, what kind of coffee he likes,
and if he repairs the hail damage himself when the storms
come through in the spring.
I'll ask him what I need to learn before I can have his
position when he retires.

Because I want to believe
that's all there is to it,
to knowing what to do with loneliness;
we have to watch each other's extras spaces
and make sure they don't get hurt or too big.

Protect

I have swallowed the cardboard,
chewed it to a pulp and gulped
it down. It tasted like stale
dirt, and chemicals. Scabbed my tongue—
a hard pill to swallow.

The lump stayed in my throat,
through the flight and back to Dallas
through my body dissolving.
It made my limbs creaky and slow—
a hard pill to swallow.

And through the hospital it stayed,
the world of soft blankets and voices.
I stood flimsy and moist. My eyes grew
at the sight of you, small, ill-kept.
A hard pill to swallow

because when you swallow with eyes
nothing can wash it down. Unblinking,
the nurses sit and stare at their phones,
here only to watch the risk. They give
a hard pill. To swallow,

I hold up water in a plastic cup, because
your arms are useless in bandages.
They look like dead crabs. I try to give
you shelter, but I am made out of cardboard—
a hard pill to swallow.

(Little Structures)

This almond is like a canoe,
you said, or the shape we make
when we spoon face-to-face.
The shapes only look fragile.
Just a few almonds were crushed
at the bottom of the bag,
and to devour, your molars have to
squeeze and squeeze
to get that first pop.
So too canoes.
The explorer is encased
in what he needs
even if there's rapids or rocks.
If we were very small
and had toothpicks,
we could carve this almond into a canoe,
with benches face-to-face,
to go where the sprinkler is finicky.
Wouldn't that be something?
Why don't you see?
(But I do see, and I can't.)
(I have known about keeping safe.)
(I, too, make little structures)
(to forbear the rush of love.)

Hollow

The week my cat left, I thought a lot about straws,
how difficult it is to quantify a loss.
It doesn't feel right to say, This loss weighs
fifteen pounds, leads to less purring and vomit
on my favorite book. You had asked me once
how many holes a straw has,
and I automatically said Two.
One at the beginning, one at the end.
You said No, it's just the one hole, the
place the straw is not. My house
shrinks now, the ottoman (still gray with fur), bed,
rug where she learned how to play are all
the same: just places things are not.
But someone else said, No, straws have three,
one on each end and the hole connecting them.
He was joking, but one hole doesn't seem like,
the right answer. Holes don't have two openings
the way a straw must. And indeed,
this absence was what connected us most that week,
searching the neighborhood and woods together.
A third person said it's none, a straw has no holes
—a tube is just a conduit—
after all. A cat from an animal hoarder.
She hid in my cupboard when I first got her,
then a fat, affectionate beast, to wherever she is now.
I gave that cat a good cat life, for two years at least,
I have to tell myself, because regardless of debates about
straws, I feel a bit hollow, all the way through.

The Camera

the camera does not speak english

it concerns itself
with the
ellipses
on my face
that drip when i
am tired the exclamation point
in the middle that cannot seem to catch
a breath
the
red
question mark
bit in its corner

i pick it up i point its eyemouth
towards me
i press *flash*

and then i stop thinking with words.

Baker

From out my backseat window, I see a sign go by;
We Bake Memories,
it says. The truck has a picture of bread,
in a bag and already sliced,
with a blonde girl in pigtails who's smiling.

It all makes perfect sense.
This is a service people would want.
Most of the time, when we remember, the memories
come out in spasms
and gasps, not in a neat little package, in manageable parts
that can be consumed or stored away as needed.
The truck is large and unwieldy, filled with equipment,
I imagine, to do the work
of transporting things in your head and in your heart into
the oven, glowing like the lights they use to show x-ray
transparencies on.

I haven't heard of such a thing before,
but I guess it's not surprising because things are different
in Van Wert, Ohio than they are in Duncanville, Texas.
The houses are more spread out,
and the people seem to have slower ideas.
I haven't been here very long. It's just a week-long
business trip, and it has no business being in the Midwest.

I wonder if the driver likes his job,
out here in fields of dying yellow.
It's simple enough, I imagine,
going house to house, making stops for the folks that
have an appointment.
The truck finagles its way in front of farm houses,
the driver gets out and unloads his equipment onto a dolly.
He has longstanding customers, and he gets to know them
over the years. He asks about their children and
grandchildren and knows who makes the best lemonade.
He says *Time to begin,* and the customer sits in front of
their oven. Diodes connect the temples to the ovens,
and there's a whirl and a hum. Then, the smell of memories
fill the little houses, and the customer almost always gives
a smile of relief.

This isn't a job I could do, as pleasant as it sounds.
For one thing, I couldn't drive a big eighteen wheeler like that.
I used to get panic attacks while driving around Dallas, Texas,
which, granted, sounds pretty reasonable, given how people
drive there. But the panic attacks were bad and once led to
wrong-way driving.
The panic attacks were dangerous and
would get me lost on highways and in my head.
I couldn't breathe or pull over or stop. My brain
would get all ashy, my palms sweaty,
and I would try hitting my head until I
could think, just think again.

That's why I smoke when I drive
—to remind me that things are real, really real,
going into and out of my lungs,
and that it's not all flotsam and random memories,
coming in spasms and gasps.

I haven't had a panic attack in while,
so that's an improvement. I figured out the GPS on my
phone, which is helpful. It reminds me that things
are here and now and existing in the present.
The last one I had was a few months ago,
on my way home from therapy. I thought:
What if when I have kids, I hurt them too?
Because I don't think when he was twenty-five,
my father ever thought he would either.
My head got scattered like breadcrumbs, and I wasn't
home until after dark, pretending to myself that I could
be this neat little package, in manageable parts.

I'm bad enough as a passenger.
Working in insurance claims does that.
Makes you worry that your driver doesn't pay enough
attention to the truck ahead of him or will attempt
a u-turn or miss his exit.
Right now, in Van Wert, Ohio, I'm particularly anxious.
We're on our way to the airport, my coworkers and I,
and I don't want to miss our flight. I want to get back to Texas.
My home is there. A home without memories of childhood,
a home to grow *into* instead of *up* in.

And I think that means something,
this anxiety and need to leave and go somewhere else.
I've never been homesick before.
I have a house now, in Duncanville, Texas.
It's a little shabby and could use some fixing up.
But my books and cats and roommate are there.
My rugs that get lumpy. My front door knob you have to jiggle.
The windows that don't let enough light in and are drafty.
My parents criticized that when they visited at the beginning
of last summer, after I had first bought it.
They haven't been back since.

And I wonder if the *We Bake Memories* truck
will ever make it to the metroplex in Texas.
Maybe I'll call the driver up and make an appointment.
He'll finagle his truck up my dirt driveway and come in.
He'll like my house and think a little unexpected breeze is nice.
He'll connect my temples up to the diodes and to the oven.
It'll glow like an x-ray on a light. And I won't be afraid of it
the way I'm afraid to get a real x-ray because of the bone
fractures it might show.

After an hour or so, the memories will be done, all of them,
from years and years of abuse and addiction and joy, too.
It'll make sense. A nice, neat package, where things will stay
where they belong. My whole house will smell like bread.
I'll use an old shirt—I've lost the oven mitts—
and take out the loaf. Once it's cooled down, the driver will say,
Here, won't you please share with me?

Fly Away Home

I dream of ladybugs at 39,000 feet.
My wrists are cut. No blood.
As if in a stop-motion movie, they come
teeming—delicate, awkward, each with their own mind.
I remember later that ladybugs mean good luck,
and I could use some luck coursing through my veins
instead of your DNA.

But we had luck that day at the lake, twenty odd
years ago—the tan tackle box usurped by a swarm
of the smallest ladybugs I would ever see,
except for the ones in my dreams. My small
fingers and your large ones nimbled
around them to get to neon bait. You threaded
the hook, too sharp for an excited girl. I caught
two fish that day. You took a photo,
me with that prize. You were proud, then.

Now, you are too sharp to be around.
You got your hooks in my blood good.
DNA for abuse and illness that might
take its course someday.
But that day, if it comes, cannot undo
that picture you have in your hallway still
of a squealing girl with two dead fish—
delicate, awkward, with my own damn mind.

Poem for My Sisters

Think of a paper-cut.
That familiar, small annoyance
that somehow pulses up your arm,
that hope it won't catch
on cloth and dirt.

That is what my childhood is like—
a sting under the surface of things.
And it caught this morning in my door-frame
when I saw my acre of land pooling in the rain,
the mud from a shoe print on the porch.

And I remembered in brown blurs
six grubby hands digging and sculpting
good mud in my parents' backyard
from almost two decades ago.

We were over by the moss-patches,
under the kitchen window. We made it
through the rosebushes, somehow,
back when our mother tended them assiduously,
(back when she could be assiduous about anything).
We made three mounds and patted them,
proud of our secret work.

Claire said that pies need spices.
She was eight and knew things like that.
I said I would get them from the kitchen
because I was the one that knew about sneaking.
Sarah said not to get caught.

When I returned with jars of cinnamon, basil,
nutmeg, and lots of cloves,
Claire said to take just enough
to make good pie but not to be noticed.
Sarah was nervous about me getting the jars messy
and that would give us away
the next time our father cooked.

But, still, we were all delighted
and pressed firmly the cloves and basil
into the tops and then sprinkled cinnamon and nutmeg,
our pies made sweeter from stealing.

I forget sometimes that you, too, now
have similar sluices on your fingertips.
I forget sometimes that you, too, watched
a backyard eat itself alive when trees fell in
and tools turned themselves to garbage,
I forget you, too, saw the toilet disintegrate by
the back porch
from when our father put it out there right around
the time we stopped inviting guests.

I forget you, too, saw the weeds last Christmas,
now up to five feet tall, some with roots and thorns.
... But I like to imagine that beneath them somewhere
are three mud pies, still smelling of basil and cloves.

The Weight of Skin

Your desire is to be fleshless.
The scars cluster too meaningfully like constellations.
There has to be a latch in the back that can be undone,
if only you knew how to reach it.

It would be like peeling a mango--
hard shell sliding over sticky shoulders.
And later, the more delicate parts,
the toes and fingers, like pulling paper
off old taffy. And then—

leave it. Leave it for the garbageman to ponder.
Leave like a deflated, white balloon.
The skin had the weight of years.

How the Light Gets In

1.

I am standing in the burnt-up home,
trying to learn how to love America.

I'm in Lima, OH for an on-the-site training.
Insurance adjuster, with boots and clipboard.

The contractor tells me about the chemical sponges
they are using to clean up smoke. Industrial blowers for
the non-porous materials, huge drying fans for
the damage the fire-department did.

So much has to be thrown away.
Cheap vinyl flooring (the cheapest you can get)
baseboard, carpet, drywall.
I can see the studs, jack and king.
cripple studs, and rafters.
Thoroughly gutted, it's an umbrella that will protect no one.

2.

We climb up on the roof too, the contractor and I,
and I feel like I'm climbing onto the back of a beached whale.
So high up with nothing to hold me.
At my feet, the roof is gray, scabbed,
strange, dry barnacles.

Everyone neglects apartment roofs,
The contractor tells me.
It's out of sight, out of mind.
The roof was badly damaged, even before the fire.
Years of neglect
to the parts people
don't think about but need.

It's a standard built up roof,
layers of asphalt that get cracked
in snow and sun.
Smog gets trapped in the environment and eats.
Anything reflective will damage the roof,
and there's a light in everything; that's how the cracks get in.

3.

You'll have to forgive me for misquoting
Leonard Cohen's song *Anthem*. He died
yesterday, and that was the day after elections,
when I had no choice but look at burnt up homes.

4.

I don't know all the words to Anthem,
but I do know *Pledge of Allegiance*.
I learned it in school. Here it is again:

*I pledge allegiance to the flag of the United States of
America, and to the Republic for which it stands, one
Nation under God, indivisible, with liberty and justice for all.*

5.

Whatever caused the fire, the cleaning is largely the same.
Maybe meat was left on the stove too long,
or a fuse shorted out in a computer or lamp.
Maybe the insulation in the attic was too sparse,
or, more likely, too much to save on the heating bill.

The chemical sponges are to clean up smoke.
Industrial blowers for the non-porous materials,
huge drying fans for the damage the fire-department did.

And then, the finishing touches, during the rebuild.
Spray on mold killer, Pine-Sol for the new floors, Pledge.

Whatever caused the fire, the cleaning is largely the same,
all of us backs bent over, masks to keep us safe,
singing *Alleluia* under our breaths.

Birds of Ill-Repute

For Matthew Haines, road warrior with heart of gold.

I said you reminded me of turkey buzzards,
and you received it as a compliment, thank God.
Because they are not unlovely birds,
sitting in groups in lifeless trees like gargoyles
to keep the bad spirits away.
You camped in my backyard for a week,
in summer in Texas, no less,
unobtrusively reading and writing and
smoking my cigarettes, circling quietly
around my house, from the backyard to the porch.
Buzzards get a bad reputation through
hovering above, sniffing out gaseous decay,
and picking at the left overs in a jerky, bloody dance.
But I think people forget that buzzards
feed their young through regurgitation.
They must find what's serviceable and still good
to help someone smaller,
who doesn't yet have silver feathers for flight.

At Shell Station

I like things that look like garbage but aren't,
says the woman behind the counter
at the Shell Station on Wheatland and Clark Road,
in Duncanville, Texas.
That's why I put all these hermit crabs back here.
And indeed, behind the gum, the counter top, the wall
of cigarettes, is a beach and an ocean that goes on and on,
and on that beach are dozens of hermit crabs of varying
sizes and colors. *Come take a look,* she says,
and I put down the Dr. Pepper, Butterfinger, and
Kamel Red 100s I was buying and
go behind the counter.

The sand is piled up nicely and feels strange in my
high-heeled shoes and office-appropriate skirt.
There's a breeze, and this ocean smells just as it should
—salt, fish, wild.
And the crabs are forming a little chain
and changing out in rapid succession.
The biggest one goes into a discarded conch shell,
the second biggest one goes into that one's shell,
the third biggest goes into the second,
the fourth into the third,
and so on and so forth.
Hermit crabs really do that.
It's on Wikipedia, you can look for yourself.

The rest of the story so far is just some bullshit I made up.
I've never been to that particular Shell Station, but I
imagine that it's more or less the same as all the other
gas stations around these parts:
smelling of antiseptic with lights that buzz and flicker.
I don't even wear heels; I'm too clumsy,
and my tits and ass stick out just fine on their own,
which is why high-heeled shoes were invented in the first
place.

I guess I made that up because I want to believe
there's a place where you can see prepositions
behave as strangely as they do in my head.
What I mean is, think of a hermit crab in relationship
to a shell it has found.
It's in the shell because it inhabits the shell.
But also, it is the shell. Without it, it would die.
And in the same way, I am in my head,
with its anxieties and dumb ideas,
but also I am my own head.
It's not like mind / body distinction is terribly real anyways.
I inhabit my mental illness like a hermit looking for the right
cave or shell—but I'm not just these feelings, these doubts,
these fears, right?

And with that thought comes a similar anxiety—
how I am looked at as someone with illness.

I've been looked over, looked through, looked down on,
and, on occasion, looked up to.
But when someone looks at you—at—things getcomplicated.
You accuse them, late at night, naked, in bed, of using all sorts
of incorrect prepositions: of looking onto you, upon you,
about you, inside you.
And you know it's bullshit,
but you accuse anyways because you're scared.

People have told me that prepositions are purely idiomatic,
and they don't really make a difference.
But I think they're wrong about / in / with regard to / that.
It's just that prepositions make me scared and worried that
I'll run and lead to rolling over and hiding in / under /
between / through blankets.

It's not that prepositions don't matter;
just that they behave oddly.
Like these hermit crabs switching out these shells they inhabit
and are. They run sidewise, like you'd expect, and can't talk
about things head-on, and dodge and evade,
and make up stories, and hide in / within / between /
amongst sand.

The chain of dozens of crabs has finished its course,
and the smallest shell is left on the beach,
tenant moved to a more well-suited home and self.
The woman who works there hands me the shell,
and I cup it in both palms.

And I don't know what I'm looking at:
abandoned home, too-small clothes, part of a body.
But maybe at Shell Station,
things don't have to get
pedantic or idiomatic or solipsistic but just are.

It's a small shell, the size of my thumb nail.
It is blue.
It has a good weight.

I stand up from squatting to leave,
shell in my right hand, sand in my too-high heels,
and the woman stands up too. She turns to me.
Her gray eyes go on and on, like an imaginary ocean.
She says, *When you are seen, really seen, looked at,*
no one sees garbage,
just the is not.

The Pear

You tried explaining pears,
how the grit in the skin is
what distinguishes them from apples,
as well as not floating in water,
and that the perfect one will fit
in the palm like a bird resting
with its neck between the thumb and forefinger,
and how right is the feel, but
to balance it on a counter, a bowl
is needed to prevent toppling.

You tried to tell me of their ripeness,
how if I bite too early, it tastes
shrunken and recoiled, and the rest
is bitter, whether I force my way
through it or throw it away, and biting too late
makes mangled tendons in the dish. You tried
explaining the rarity in gathering weight,
why pears are beautiful when
you take care and notice the grit.

Poem for D.H.

I want to be intensely soft,
the way you are with me.
The way you took me
when I was all corners
and addicted to sharp edges,
and gathered me into origami,
folded me on your bed with you,
when I was too drunk and afraid of myself
to even take off my boots.
I put my head on your chest, smelling
the t-shirt your mom gave you.

I want to be intensely soft,
the way the light was the day
we processed like school children
to the place his memorial was,
and I finally made you smile.
Behind us was his widow, your fiancée,
who pondered your strange college friend,
who covers up the need to cry
with jokes and endless cigarettes.

I want to be intensely soft,
the way you will be when
you become father to two little girls
he left behind. Intense and soft,
like a river that has no bottom.

Dirt with Bits

I, too, have seen the mud
and was unsure how it got here.
Some is around the front of the house
which reminds me of food left on dirty dishes.
(I think it was your feet that smeared it.)
There are puddles also, over by the footpath,
causing the damp dirt around them
to stick up in tiny points. They make our whole
yard look pimply and adolescent.
But most of the mud lies under the palms of blue stones,
waiting like a bed already made.

After lifting up the largest stone,
I plunge my left index-finger in;
it's at least two knuckles deep.
The mud has the coolness of clean sheets
but none of its crispness.
And from what I can tell, shadow, mulch,
and dirt caught with bits
of cigarette ash and insects
then all splattered from a faulty sprinkler
is what makes the mud maculate and fecund.

We made it, and it was already here.
On its surface is the beginnings of moss,
and at its base is love.

Dead Pangolin Lullaby
for Jeanette Powers

What good is armor for those that die
inside it? This creature looked so whimsical and fierce,
like a bear trapped inside an artichoke,
but for a snout and tongue betraying something other.
The pangolin's armor, which had held such subtle
movement and oddly balanced grace,
proved futile and now a sort of cage.

We must think, then, of its uses
for those left behind. Overlaid like shingles,
they could be made a sort of house.
A shelter from years of learning fierceness
and oddly balanced grace. Or perhaps
the shape suggests leather mollusks.
We can use endurance when nothing else will thrive.

Up close, the scales have ridges,
like a workman's finger, turned into leather
from use. Perhaps we can use the scales
when our hands give out, making ourselves
larger to do what we must. And a step back
reveals the pangolin is barked like a hickory tree.
It can help us breathe.

I have to believe that even if my toughness
cannot save me, it will still matter
somehow to those left behind.
It will help someone breathe.
Your grandfather had said the best
time to plant a tree is twenty years ago.
The second best time is now.

The Operation

Father,
I said,
Father, I'm sorry.
I've looked for God everywhere, but I don't understand.
I don't need to see His face,
but I do need a sign.

I mean, do you think God is like some
some missing child, and we should all just watch Amber
Alerts—hah!—religiously and buy every milk carton in
the country, like He just got borned and fled, and we are
all Herod except we don't want to kill him, just say hi?

Do you think God is sending out subliminal messages
in all those spy movies, and He's secretly telling us
Act
Like
This?
Like, like, it'll be difficult and top-secret, and you'll
have to go undercover in your classrooms and in your
boardrooms, you'll have to infiltrate the masses, but
Fear
Not.
I've given you all the high-tech gear you need. And and
and and I've given you magical bread you can get at
convenient times and locations throughout the city,
and I've given you the televangelists.

And oh! there's this book, see, full of top-secret code …
And then God'll hint during the briefing that, yeah,
He's sorry He's made doing His bidding
so damn inconvenient,
but we simply cannot afford to let this kind of
information fall into the wrong hands.
Or, um, He's wanted in seven countries and really doesn't
wish to get captured again.
That's why His number's unlisted.

No, I will not calm down.

I said, Do you mean when you say
Find God
like God like God like is is is three letters to be circled in
a field of other random letters,
the peanut butter at the end of a maze—I guess that
makes us all rats—like God is
the right answer to a multiple choice question,
with Buddha and Allah
as other options?

But I've I've I've I've I've I've looked, Father, I've looked
anyways. Over hill and over dale.
I looked in all the right images.
The sheep smelled like sheep, and the shepherd, well,
he wasn't Good;
he shouted
what in God's name was I doing there, standing amidst
his sheep.

I said, good question.

The crucifix has the same emotional significance to me
as the American flag.
I want to salute it as it looms over us,
and I think it would be a nice touch at baseball games.
And as for light and darkness—
how many times were you told as a kid not to stare
into the sun?

And God's supposed to be here, right, right in this room,
but with your face. Which I find odd.
Don't you see that there's a fence between us?
There is a Berlin wall.

The priest said,
Nadia,
he said,
Nadia, maybe you should look inside yourself.

So when I got home, I did.

The first thing I saw was my ribcage,
held close,
like a spidery baby.
My liver wrapped around like a slimy sweater.
Then, my stomach tucked away, almost out of sight,
like a memory
still moist and quivering.

I saw my ascending colon with its clusters of congealed eyes.
My small intestine,
nestling on top of itself like a family of cats
Then, my bladder,
red and pulsating like lips stretched over a bottle.
I saw my hip bone is connected to my thigh bone.

Now hear the word of the Lord

Paradise

The whole thing is overrated.
I mean, it's not bad as far as Indian buffets go,
but I was expecting something rather more.
The food can be tepid, and everyone knows
Indian food is best when it's piping hot.
But there's a mango custard, and the color is unbelievable,
like a sunrise on a desert,
and it's sweet and chunky and pure.

I got food poisoning from eating at Paradise once,
or some kind of upset. There was a liquid incident
in the bathroom at work. I guess I keep coming back
because of the location, not because I think it's anything
special. The buffet is at Kiwest and MacArthur
in Irving, Texas, and that's right where my office is.
It's nice to walk to lunch
when you only have forty-five minutes.

All in all, though, you would think Paradise would be
more crowded, despite its obvious mediocrity.
There's a lot of offices in this part of Irving,
and everyone likes to leave their tiny cubicle now and then.

I'm not sure what I did to deserve to end up in dingy-lit,
aromatic buffet and other people did not. I thought for sure
I'd see some of the past greats, like Mother Theresa or
Gandhi or George Harrison or someone.

I'm not a particularly good person. I mean,
I know I could work wonders on seventy-two virgins,
but that's someone else's idea of paradise and not here.
I never thought I'd end up in that other place, just not Paradise.

Paradise—the great reward, the prize at the end of a chess
match, what we strive for, our just desserts,
which is mango custard, because that shit is delicious,
I'm telling you.

I was told I would end up the other place,
though, on more than one occasion.
Priests when I confessed to stabbing myself with a pocket knife
in wrists and feet. They said if I didn't pray to baby Jesus for
forgiveness for making a gross parody of Christ's redemptive
act, I'd go to hell.
My only question for them was, why baby Jesus?
Is regular, grown-up Jesus not enough?

My parents said that too, in an email,
because I wasn't a virgin.
They said Jesus didn't value me the way those men clearly did,
because if a man wanted to sleep with you, that meant he only
valued you because of what you could do between your legs.
But I think it's only my parents who think of me that way,
in terms of what I do with my vagina.

I don't tell my therapist that, not really.
He's Jungian, not Freudian, but nonetheless,
he might have a field day with that remark.

I never believed the priest and my parents.
About me going to hell, I mean.
I'm very charismatic when there's something on the line
and bet I could talk my way out of it.

Nonetheless, I didn't think I'd go to Paradise—
even if the scriptures were misleading and Paradise is a
tepid Indian buffet in the bourgeoisie part of Irving, Texas.
I don't think I've done enough to really earn it.
I'm selfish, impatient, and a little insecure.

Actually, that's not true. I was quoting those basic bitches
who pretend Marilyn Monroe has deep insight into the
human condition.
But my quote was ironic, which makes it clever.
And for another thing, I actually do know exactly why I'm here,
and part of that verse paragraph was a lie.

I had spent a whole session with my therapist
talking about my parents.
This was my idea.
I was sure he gets lots of patients who say that their parents
are crazy, so I said no, really, my parents are crazy and that
we were going to spend the next session talking about it.

At the start, I said that when I was a kid, I wasn't allowed
to cough. By the end, he believed me.

He asked, *Well, how do you think you survived?*
and I had to think about it.
I told him I think I survived because of my imagination,
that I would pretend I was somewhere else,
an adult with credit cards and a car or on an alien spaceship
or dead.

But the problem now is, I keep doing it.
I keep pretending not to be where I am.
I'm absent.
I deliberately misinterpret signs and take them for wonders.

And now I'm in a booth with torn leather in Paradise,
finishing my second bowl of mango custard and thinking
Is this really all there is?

I eat too much, as usual, and contemplate how fat I'm getting
and how one day, I won't be able to get in this booth anymore,
and that's how I won't be welcomed into Paradise:
by getting too fat.
I waddle to the entryway where the register is and fish out
my debit card.

If this is Paradise, then the man at the register is an angel
who would sing at me or tell about God's glory
or how God loves even His lost children.
But the man says *Everything was good?*
And I say *Yeah* because I don't know what else to say.

He doesn't impart some wisdom
or infuse anything with meaning or special grace.
He makes less than minimum wage and doesn't give a shit
about me or my dining experience.
Behind the register, though, the wall is mirrored,
and I catch myself. Because when you take away the artifice,
the memories, the word games, the constructs,
the wishing for places loneliness can go
or places where memories make sense,
or places to get clean,
or where prepositions are embodied,
there is nothing left to do but look at yourself.

I've gained weight,
I have scars.
My lipstick is smeared,
and I have curry on my sweater.
But I don't need anyone—real or imaginary—
to tell me where or what I am.
I have my whole person. I survived.

Phenology

These walls must
have lungs. How
else to explain

the sensation of expansion
and contraction
the fast the slow.

Love
you have soft eyes
but with sharp

cheekbones.
I explore everything
that throbs above

me with my thumbs
pressing temples
in finding

how to not unfasten
hair at the roots
and these walls
must have their own
lungs. How else to
explain the rhythm.

Prayered

I.

I have anxiety about the nouns in the past. No language I know of has them. Verbs, of course, are the things with tense. This stands to reason. An action can be done. When it is over, it is complete. Gone and complete synonymous. I loved badly. I planted weeds. I wept often. Actions sealed in tubes, immutable. You gave me earrings, once, and worried they were too small. Turtles stamped into sterling silver — I have sensitive ears — and sealed in a case.

And what of it? One will wander off, given the way I am with earrings. Gone, but could you say, properly speaking, complete? Earringsed. For now, I keep both on either side of my enormous head. I tap them to make sure they are there.

II.

After Chernobyl, scientists plant sunflowers to absorb radiation, and the results are inconclusive. It seems too beautiful not to be true and too beautiful to be. You can picture it if you try — scientists bent over in yellow hazmat suits. Kneeling as if in prayer, planting the start of undoing.

Trying to undo a loss, even if in vain, must be good, must matter. The sunflowers, we know, cannot bring back the dead, extract the cancer, or de-scorch the building. But still, a sort of haphazard blessing on the nouns of the past.

III.

And that, I think, is why people pray. To bring blessing on the things gone but not complete. I heard you once, through the walls—I have sensitive ears—weeping. You never cry. I heard and did nothing. I covered my head with my pillow. Awful sound like alarms. I froze, parts of me getting smaller in halves. I can be a shitty friend to live with. I'm sorry. But now years later, it's probably stupid, but I might have it in me, to pray, just a little, for those sobs through the wall.
They filled the air like flames.

Epaino
For Kerstin

I assumed it wouldn't happen to you,
dying I mean. You dwell where ruins lie—
in museums or pasted flat in textbooks.
When someone is from antiquity,
they are forever in the historical present.
You have no business being dead.
Writing this, I had to look up some basics.
I was most likely your worst student. After
I graduated, you forgave me and said keep
writing. I understand poetry better now,
which is staggering in its absurdity. You
taught me Sappho, Lucretius, Ovid. I turn
now to Wikipedia, school books long gone.
Minerva is the goddess of wisdom and owls.
Elysium is where souls go, if they are brave and true.
There does not seem to be consensus
among the ancients about placing the gods
and heroic souls. But what I imagine is this:
Minerva departs to Elysium too.
Her soul is the size of an owl.
A voice from the grove says Rest
now. So many students have crowded
under your wings. Now, it is your turn.
I know this is insufficient, and I've always
been bad at translation.

It's just a story, a myth I am making while trying
to be true. I am no Orpheus, just someone
who assumed you would not,
die, I mean. But I'm not going to apologize.
I am learning to thank instead. Thank you
for teaching us to be ourselves without flinching.

Tapetum Lucidum

I.

We ask animals what the language of grief is, and think they know. Dumb, heavy things feel like they would know. Look into this cow's eye. Can you capture it? You cannot. The *tapetum lucidum* escapes all but the newest cameras, and even those photos are rudimentary.

A iridescence over the iris, something other creatures have that we do not. It helps the beasts see at night.

II.

One night, I dream the eyes have secrets that we forget every time we draw them. Instead of one iris in each eye, we have a second slightly smaller one that bobbles in the outer corner. In my dream, I look into yours. The second iris is cloudy with glaucoma. All the second irises are.

III.

In the Swiss Alps, at night, mysteriously, on three separate occasions, the cattle hurl themselves off a cliff. Each morning, the farmer finds them and calls helicopters to retrieve the corpses, lest they taint the ground water. There are no predators here, no sea to leap into.

The cows lived there and could see well enough.
They pile up after, like scrambled eggs, indistinguishable from one another.

Cows move in herds, and must be led to really get anywhere. Imagine. Imagine being the first of your species to end your own life.

The Language of Fruit Trees

Poems by Abigail Beaudelle

Hypnagogic Hymn

A songbird
seeks Orpheus
in the depths of a
cave
hollowed
in a split
melon seed —
starts at the sound of
strings.

Dream I

sleep 11pm woke 7:44 had a dream about smuggling drugs in cleaned out rabbit kidneys and accidentally dosing myself orally and topically - felt hot/fiery, then warm numbness.

Forest Fire — Mystery

I dip my finger in Bacchus's cup
poison to redefine my perception
of the color orange
bright swatch brushed against my
vision to
forever be the core of this color

caution
sunset
citrus
all bells in alarm
alien
oriole
the sunburned shoulder of God

there is a fire in the sacred grove
each synapse an aching tree
I
clasp my trembling hands.

Dream II

very sad sick outdoor marine world aquarium in midwest. piranhas, rainbow trout, seals, lots of algae. old woman displays the fish — she drains the tank and puts on the lights. in one of the tanks there's a beet that has been grown as a bonsai. the 300 year old beet contains the souls of the marine life.

Lioness Song

i.
I move my leg in lion's leg
my breath ripples
her breath
skin, acacia-crossed
pins tree shadows
to my soul —
we walk healed
with the memory of old wounds

every long grass blade
wagging
tongue of trauma

ii.
peripheral flickers
flocky black-lip
dust-mawed
we pant fear
vaporize oil heat/terror
sunset scampers
underfoot
and re-forms —
a godhead at our back

iii.
dream parallel
already
already
deja vecu waker
hallelujah

iv.
in the lioness
I sleep
lengthwise

Dream III

dream about worms with whip-like tails infesting my arm; cut them out and broke the first still in skin — poison tail like a jellyfish tentacle — burning white translucent thread. second attempt — wind worm around a stick, it becomes the rod of Asclepius.

Helix
for Allyson

The snake curls in on itself
Allyson says quietly to no-one.
Outside the seedlings snicker
and chirp to each other like song
birds.

Soon, we eat raisin bran with plastic
spoons. Crushed flakes whorl —
the creation of time.
We talk about cartoons
when a new sun filters in on Monday.
She wears a blanket on her head like a
habit.

I give my heart to your heart
she says between bites
at four she
conceives of love
visceral. A tangible circulation —
two burning hearts,
a thorn surround.

She wants to watch a movie.
She can see her face in the back
of a Looney Tunes DVD.

A mirror caged in rainbow.
I think of the Phantom Palace —
a spirit helix
turns in on itself.

Caduceus
Snail
Oroboros
Isopod
Eddy
Ivy

I return to myself
openly

Dream IV

there was an intricate ivory-colored cup featuring a carved nativity, and a slice taken out of a burdock root.

another dream featured horses. I had the ability to teleport.

Basil

Your pagoda
chatters
skyward,
a muttered prayer
repeated in terminal leaves

Shall I sit
bare-minded
in this temple?
Oil radiates
the scent of the sun

Dream V

bought Mexican beer at a small shop — the cashier was an old lover, but I did not remember her name. in the past she had given me a tattoo (left hand, just above middle knuckle, b & w eyes), and showed me her latest — four dots in a triangle underneath her tongue.

Midwestern Woods Haiku 1-5

For Bill Gainer, with love & apologies

i.
Near crippled television sets
mushrooms
copulate & drip
over downed trees —
fresh ink.

ii.
A pair of glasses
upright
wedged between
earth & sky.

iii.
On the ground —
the signs.
Above me —
one ripe mulberry!

iv.
Under the leaves
of the mayapples,
only a lone golfball.

v.
Old Ash pile —
the broken head
of a lawn ornament angel
looks earthward.

Interlude
Allyson Johanson, Age 4
for her Father

we have to find dad
his glasses are frozen in the pond
my daddy is in a cage

we have to get our masks
there's a Jaguar in the woods
and we have to scare it with our masks

Dream VI

I was driven back home — wrong turn took us to the ocean. inland, a road that looked like rural Japan — mossy stone walls, a constellation of ponds. catfish crawled from the banks into the water, and we stopped for awhile. I jumped into the pond and was bitten by a poisonous catfish called 'group lover catfish' — extreme pain, swelling of hand, face. electric bee sting feeling from many tooth punctures.

Primitive

I am a cowardly caveman
I
walk catty-corner to
common decency
gnaw the marrow out of
moonbeams
when times are leaner

Do you know the language
of fruit trees? I don't.
Call them down for me.
Let me spend a lifetime
ignorant & humble
and another lifetime
with my heart plunged
beating into the plant kingdom
let me have phyla for eyes
a cryptic taxonomy
hammered into peripheral vision
I want to lick the soil
off my hands
weave through the earth
like a psychic eel
come nose to nose with earthworms
& press my palms to dormant
rhizomes to feel the new life kicking ...

I am a throwback
groan guttural
gnash-teeth weep
at the loss of words

I will knuckledrag
back to open stars
can't drive cars
can't talk to you

Will I have something to say
when I can snare the shade
of orange that haunts my skull
like a bad-luck dog?

Will I have something to say
when the grass
shivers back into its own shape?

I don't talk too good
I don't grok too good
I love you.

My nose drips milk
onto dry earth
my feet beat rabbit
dirt when I dance
city steps

I don't know the language of motion,
of fruit trees.
I will break the bones of my own
dreamtime
reset my boundary.

I am a captive caveman
all my songs
whispered to the dirt.

Grouse-mind I will
jump when you call me —
a flash of orange
in your field of vision

Is sunset the color of a woman?
Orange-winged
I settle in the hay fields
to nest —
all stems bent
not broken.

Dream VII

lost with no money after missing a ferry to New York, I started walking to North Carolina. along the way I met a group of people roughly my own age standing outside their home. we were talking when all of a sudden the group was attacked by a rampaging bear. after being scattered and menaced, I managed to get behind the enraged bear and thumb out its eyes. I grappled the animal and broke its neck, killing the bear. we soon cleaned the bear and cooked, ate.

Exploit

1. An exciting act or action
2. To use [....] in a way that helps you unfairly.

Shopping for a phone online
80% off down
to $16USD —
it will do everything
I desire

I check the specs
it comes with an sd slot
is compatible with my favorite music player
all-new components peeled
off the skin
of child workers

I buy it anyways.
I moved 900 miles from
my mother.

Flight
is a homeopathic
pill
the earth diluted
past recognition,
no trace of active
component
left at these levels.

The chocolate in my
in-flight trail mix
tastes like ivory,
smells like
brown blood.

My life is wrapped
in exploit
am I a predator now?

My shirt and layover coffee
are both Nicaraguan.
I stir cream into my
house blend,
blow away
the screams of marmosets
with the steam —

I do not have the patience
to let it cool.

Dream VIII

*a psychic gave me a vision of the
"heart" of a blade of grass.*

*strange Oak in childhood backyard —
troop of mushrooms growing. nearby a notebook
with a drawn cartoon (alien/asemic).*

dream of mysterious illness signified by 5 black dots.

Fly in the Chapel

(with apologies to Emily Dickinson)

I felt a fly's mind when it died
the low electric thrum of a
crushed exoskeleton
run through my thumb.

Fly, did your world go pastel
when I pinched your third eye?
Did your sins run clear
the insides of you plaster
and see-through
against the kitchen
window pane?

Do you feel pain?

Fly, I miss you,
the soft ripple
of a wing beaten against
my arm —

I shiver, skin
shrinking,
flicker, the withers of a horse.

It is Saturday, I took my Sabbath
and killed you. Fly
so much cream —
orange, a red speck.
Dead now,
you are my stained glass
meditation —
a window to God.

Dream IX

found myself in the woods at night trying to protect three children from a mountain lion, watched the mountain lion get gored repeatedly by a white tail deer buck.

Eight is For Grief

Five is for riches,
Six is a thief.
Seven, a journey,
Eight is for grief.
  - Old English folk-rhyme

i.
When is
your baby due
she asks
in line at KFC she is
slum-bellied with
a face of hard rain,
her husband
a long monolith
by the register.

I wish I could have
babies again —
(she speaks as if
praying into the rain)

    I wanted eight.

(The monolith shifts —
a boulder on the mountainside
anticipating
Sisyphus.)

ii.
Behind her Colonel
Harland Sanders
passes out black and white
fried chicken
to Chinese children
in a photograph from 1959

Unlike her he
has achieved
his godhead

set his feet upon
the firmament
spread his arms across
oceans —
his face a buoyant light
in darkness
lesser deity
of the American Strip Mall
Pantheon,
bows to no one.

iii.
The woman in line
at KFC
tells me she could have
made it work,

dares me to defy her
with a gorgon look.
She
wants to be the Night
0
or deep space
voluptuous and heavy as horses
with the oyster spat
of stars.

She
has made herself her own
Virgin Mother and
having borne five children still
dreams of birthing titans
to carry her
from this place.

Dream X

dreamed of trying to find beach front property. visited a hotel to find out later that the hotel put on a nightly show using their captive gorilla to impersonate Elvis. inauspicious dream sequence — guitar broken, rabbits dead, poverty stricken, visions of hell.

Motherhood

My mother said it best —
we never know the meaning
of the word *vulnerability*
until the definition is placed in our arms.

Every single one
of my bulldog-whip reactions
the end-product of fear.

I can't walk out of my house
on my own anymore.
I haven't been able to for three
months since the last of my tomatoes
failed to ripen
rotting green on the vine.

*

Two days ago I heard a knock
at the door too late — in my
pajamas I dashed down the stairs
to find the building's maintenance man already
three steps inside my home.
We stared at each other,
madhaired.

He waved the blue furnace filter
like a press-pass.

Allyson, two years old,
cried upstairs from being left
unexpectedly.

I told him I could change it
and he left.

**

motherhood

is a muzzling.
The rippling outward of
trickle-down economics-styled
fear tactics.

Fuck the Patriot Act
the perception of everyday
scrutiny is excruciating.

Every voiced opinion
contains
the potential
of devolving to a rifle range
and 0.8:1
guns to Americans

is a pretty high
ratio.

***

I peeled an orange for my daughter.
we're working on the word *please*.
At two years old
owning an orange slice
is a cause for joy.
The curl of orange peel
becomes a frog in small hands
hops across my desk —
LOOK mom look —
Frog

Ribbit Ribbit!

Dream XI

dreamed last president and vice president were attacked in their airplane by someone riding a dragon. dreamed two alien species (both robotic drones/suits) landed on earth, one tore the other apart. my mom collected children's toys.

Mother's Day, 2017

For Michaeline, my mother

A cut lemon dries on
my mother's counter.
I can't remember the name
of the nut pastry
she makes with
scrap pie dough.
This is how we lose
pieces of ourselves.
My new neighbor shouts
Happy Mother's Day
from his truck
as he drives off —
I am struck by a
sudden sadness —
900 miles away &
I miss you.

You collected duck eggs
barefoot from
the riverbank.
I wish I could have
known you before myself.

Today is perfect —
the sun touches down
to nest —
raw gold
edges hidden
in rabbit fur.

The sky bleeds blue
to midnight
behind my mailbox.

Mom, when I was sixteen
you reminded me how I slept —
tucked feet on top of you
in summer — my body fit
between rib & shoulder blade
a murmur of consciousness
curling in on itself.

Yesterday the police officer
asked if I'd heard gunshots ... I hadn't, but
quiet, for an hour
& then the neighbors mow
lawns & a small dog
rolls in my front yard.

I am not so afraid
anymore.

Mom, you lived
in a haunted house
but step sharply
into sunlight
smell of peppermint
tea tree
the roundness of
pure soap —
you match edges and
find lost
things
& a place to put them.

I check my mailbox
on Sundays.

Dream XII

saw a newly shedded snake. pregnancy worry.

dreamed my family was looking at a new property. three buildings on property including large greenhouse & communal ritual feast space. large cook kiln /bowl & tagine. bread crust left on plates.

April Midnight

In April midnight lasts four hours.
I am holding a cup of tea
like a memorial service —
in the corner of my eye
I am holding flowers for myself.

The walls breathe,
a cloth napkin on the table
flutters like the sad sacred heart
of a broken ocean.
Two waters run parallel
in opposite directions along my
spine.
I drink nothing,
but the body remembers —
I trip on an empty stomach.

We are on the couch
The Lovers —
    one teasing a poem that won't
come,
the other tracing echoes
of an old vision
    while mushrooms wag dripping
    in a cooling cup.

        I feel all at once
        like a moonbeam fucking a rose.

That night we had sex
in our own bed
in our own house
I tried to open all compartments
for you
but this one remains shut —
three blank pieces
of paper, child's watercolor set
unused on the kitchen table.
This is not the hero's journey I remember —
I die five times
but come back only twice.

In the morning my piss
smells like ashes
In the morning my composter
eats psychedelics
In the morning I pinch flowers
from too-young tomatoes
In the morning I wear oat grass
corsages
In the morning I pour tea over
gardens in offering
In the morning I bury my
state of awareness

In the morning I find I am a new
person anyways
In the morning I tuck
crutches
back in the closet.

Dream XIII

half asleep after reading , hallucinated myself as a cottage. shelves, a pie, a table, a book, a maid.

a berry bramble.

The Kingfisher's Daughter
For Amy

They fashion themselves
the Nina, the Pinta,
the Santa Maria fearless
first explorers of your archipelago
of anguish,
converge on your shores
across a bathroom tile
Atlantic
blockade the stalls —

safe harbor for lonely hearts.
They have come to kill your native tongue
to teach you the sharp English
of their violence.

ii.
The things I know about you, Amy,
are as follows -

-you liked blue candy.

-egrets nested in the blackgold edges
  of the tear in your heart.

- you were not good at math.

- your mother is the Holy Grail of grieving.

iii.
I wish this poem was about something other
than your death, those of us left behind
are terrified of where you have gone —
unintentional martyr, what do you see?

In my yard
the Love Lies Bleeding
is in bloom.

Dream IX

skin on my hand turned cobalt blue in patches and became numb, leaden, tingling. the affected skin would turn back into my own flesh tone when I worked or massaged the hand. once I stopped the cobalt numbness would return, creeping over my skin before my eyes. someone told me that it was heavy metal poisoning.

Monday's Broth

I dreamt
of a girl raised from birth
to young adulthood
inside a tin can
in my living room - bronzed
heap of gourds
moulders
autumnally
outside — a man attacks
a tree
with a diesel spear
my mailbox hangs open,
spinning like an empty windmill
six rabbits circle
like gaseous dragons
in her tin can
the girl repeats

ii.

I attacked an airport
in 15 ft
power armor
in my living room
my toddler spells *man*
on a Sesame Street
spelling game.

She makes cookies for lunch.
Outside Missouri wind cuts
straightline —
a balmy 67 degrees before
noon on December 4th
I jet-boot
across the tarmac,
weapons check
I make chicken soup for lunch.

iii.

Outside, my garden
squats —
a pregnant rabbit
stuffs my mouth with straw.
My toddler spells *aim*
on a sesame seed app I
climb the control tower
like Donkey
Kong hydraulic power
mecha mason armor
jars line my shelf
I can chicken
carrots
bronzed gourds
August drools
into December my

butterfly bush cracks
a peaked eyelid
I moon walk across a tin can
man stands with spear
mailbox hangs open
girl dreams of noodles
smells of bone.

Dream X

I pulled back an imaginary bow and let loose, pantomiming an arrow shot directed at my husband. a bolt burst into being and buried itself into his shoulder. I dug out the projectile and ran searching for an antiseptic.

Hypnopompic Hymn

Knowledge of God
enters my left eye
ZING!

I wake up from dreams
arms
undulating like
sun —
orange
sea-fronds

my suicidal days
are numbered.

Busted Battles

Poems by Dan Provost

To my girlfriend, soon to be wife Laura Cleaves…
she puts up with me every day and is always encouraging
and beautiful…I love you!!!!

Old

And the little neighborhoods we
used to live in; children playing and
parents gossiping—life in an instant…
Not simple—1967 or 1968

Just a time—a place for the
beginning of death
and
    we
        fell
            so
                deep…

Steven Daedalus had Everything on me

But what is truth
Is truth unchanging law?
We both have truths
Are mine the same as yours?
Pontius Pilate

Steven Daedalus
Your pain has more integrity than mine…
A truth of inner…a piece of meat
within a tale of discovery—narration of broken
senses…writing a tale of systematic highs and lows…
Steven,
I do not know your game…cannot even
understand its parts…are you woven
in the finite? Destined to question everything
that strolls the sidewalk with sluttish charm
or acted with dignity?
You sought…looked for a reality within
youth of confused sublime…
My darkness is cruel, bitter days
of masked despair…
trying to find—failing to look under
hidden agendas of life…
Stephen,
I envy your empty stoicism…

A pander of adolescence abundance
not afraid to fall from grace,
keeping something, something
that I cannot grasp…
You expressed it so well but so arbitrary that
it kills me to realize I can think the same thoughts
but are unable to act upon them.

My Past Five Years

You can live your weirdness your own way.
Smoke pot, be a bum…
Sit on a couch and do nothing…
Fear the inside—the outside (both literately and figuratively)
know that you're dying and don't give a fuck.
Lack a soul, find a soul—drink alone in a corner of a bar
with a great juke box, have a cause, stare through the
window and watch the children play next door…
Think *it* is an artistic philander,
cheat, lie, tell you girlfriend that you love her…
Listen to Skynyrd…hate woman, love drugs
anticipate destruction…assassinate your being by
standing in the road, adore Jimi Hendrix, hate
the *lie* that *we, you,* us live daily.
Cross over to another emotional plane that sadly
must suffice somehow for the rest of your life.
Read philosophy, hate philosophy, end poems with lines
like Brazen Escape… hike the woods for mental stability.
Read Cormac McCarthy, cheer for losers—hate the winners,
tell yourself you don't want to be like *them*…
Maybe deep down you do. Tell the truth about
where you are, shoot heroin, cry for the bad man, hunt
for air and convince yourself that you've won bagging
the big game…search…oh yes, the search—over there,
under here, behind the curtain, through the mountains, seek

and you shall find—find what? Whose situation are you
going to take advantage of…have I used the word you
too much? Tough. I don't give a shit…Isolation, desperation,
lonely, depressed, depraved—searching for kindness by being
polite—write a book about being Martin Luther King's sheriff;
talk about nothing on the telephone—forced words, entries in a
room of blood, feel your pain you will escape in the final reel.
Watch Christ's crucifixion and see it within yourself…
trap a tackle, love a little, hate a little—did I repeat?
I don't care, smother the poor—the weak, they don't deserve it,
but it's done anyways…feel bad for those who starve—
the crippled, the misguided, the disillusioned youth…
they feel—oh yes, they feel. When the blackness shaves their
guts with a dull knife that shines our constant pain.
Pain…pain. It exists—sometimes I think it's all that exists.
Denial is so easy when you can't take the next step…
we are children of nothing…a grandiose tour through the
sickening weeds, he finds… He finds summation through a
demented lottery. She gets stoned like the Shirly Jackson
story—and the accepted; the Orpahs, the Christmas lights,
the political cabinet and the protesters…will all fade in the end—
this is a world of lies, false bravado, broken chances, broken
bottles of beer that are seen in every alleyway, byway and avenue
of hope. We turn away and more die. We are guilty as we drink
our wine…the depths of our fall never ends—it will continue
                    on and on and on
Until the dream of paradise signals no more and
little children are destined to grow up as detestable adults…

A Thought in the Snow

The little things don't matter anymore…
Breathing in air from a recent storm…
Lying in wait, looking at the clouds that form
attenable shapes and images…
No,
these are things good people adjust to
when they are torn within—or barren
only for a moment, of battle of soul…

You walk tainted, alone…
Turning up your collar to keep
away the deadening cold,
and your thoughts are of penance…
a pathetic form of forgiveness to
a spirit that is unattainable…

Not to be seen nor heard
from the legions that swell all
around you.

They see the time of day and
a moment of accepted clarity…

You see an army of nothing…
Alone.
Living.

Dying.
A quest for the steps
of a nowhere that
has been resolved
by the damned few
who's terrible escape
is all too fast
and much too sudden…

Righteous but Wrong

Hazen escape
with a touch of scotch—

Walk along the sidewalk
staggering slightly.

Tides will terminate
where the tears implant the earth.

With a stroll into the bland.

Steps cease.

World Widows

She dreamt of armies,
men who fought and bled…
different names
different guises
all tired from strife
throughout the centuries of victories and defeats
body counts told to grieving widows
whose lovers were sold a bill of goods
by entrapped loyalty their men
purged so ravenously into their soul.
The women cried, present and past
Roman widows
English widows
American widows…
World widows.
We were born to suffer, not wander
as the famous song once said…
drifting into slumber…she knows
that one will not come home…
ever.

Worcester State Grad Fair

Unsure in her slim
scared psyche…

She waits her turn to approach the hiring
insurance company table…twirling her brown
straight hair into a band of insecurity…

Pink top—long sleeves—gray hi-rider pants;
conservative and by no means trendy,

she is willing to let others go ahead
of her—obedient to let assured Monster
suits walk the corporate walk and speak
the financial terminology.

Falling through the cracks will be the story
of Ms. Timid Creature…

Waiting for no opportunity within quiet pain.

Reading J.D.
(for John Dorsey)

Reading John Dorsey
in the late afternoon…
His words of villains and loneliness
never to be told by any visitor
crossing my threshold…
I turn the pages and see
more tales of John Wayne,
Gregory Corso and the
syntax of situation.
He always gets it right, that crazy beautiful poet.
I also read John Dorsey's poetry
in the early morning hours.
Because women have been
scarce and Chinese food is
a poor substitute for companionship
at 3 AM.
Sorry John, my Little Boy beats to
daffodils of isolation.
The clock continues to tick and the
grass grows over the walkway to my
small home.
So John…keep the pen handy for sad
saps like me…who want to keep the
fire warm and the chill always handy…

Warren Haynes at 3 A.M.

3 a.m. boozy Gov't Mule music plays while
staggering words dilate in and out of a dream.

The guitar riffs bounce off walls of lonely loveliness as
one figure...one man or one woman sits at a table
pen in hand—praying to the poetry gods for the
bewilderment to be over.

And off in the distance, where even the devil won't stay, are
tales of long limit stares and showdowns that bleed the
soul of thousands who write, think and die a bit each night.

The bass player strums...
The drummer keeps the solid backbeat...

Warren Haynes breaks into another directed solo...
The Babylon Turnpike takes no prisoners

So bold.
So bold..

No God or Devil

Rattles of a realizer cannot comprehend
much within a world where ugly people
play just for keeps…
The book of acts hovers over every man who dares makes
a choice when that day marked for your end has come…
It pauses in the wind, a meteor that explores all possibilities
of pain and pleasure, eternal life or unabashed dark—
you can seek…but will you ever find? You can walk within
the spirt of God but where will you end? The apostles make
it clear in some sense, worship the Lord and you shall be saved.
My mind is clouded—a death within a world…a shame of
wanting answers…none ever come…
I am just a man.

They Are Not Friends

Colorless memories of
slapping ass with the
bony girl who's crack
addiction led her to peddle a
death that would not even
leave skeletal remains…
Yesterday, she cried
when you gave her 40
bucks…a salary of escape
to worlds of nothing; only
minutes that lived inside
a tin-foil pipe.
Tomorrow, her life story
might be on the obituary
page— not a long tale, but both of you knew
this when your uneasy liaison was
formed; however, what happens
twelve hours from now
is unimportant.
Today is now…your search
for companionship involves
a whore with six teeth missing.
Trying to convince herself she's human
but understanding her Cinderella redemption
has been accumulatively lost over years on the street.

One day at a time lives
in recovery books and
twelve step programs…
But sometimes…even the day
ain't worth living.

10 Degrees on Main South Worcester

Welfare mother bundles up
her six kids—readying them
to taste the brutish wind.

that blows the fallen
snow over steps of harsh
booze and drug addictions.

The faces on Main South, all
red and crispy; look away from
my car with jealous disgust…

After all—bad habits
should not be shared with
one who's playing Steppenwolf
songs on the CD player.

My watching them is a cheap shot, an
unmentioned kick in the groin for those
walking, freezing and scattered along
the depravity of Worcester.

This is the island of misfit
junkies and winos of the city
on display…living, but having
no place to go.

I drive away…crying for a second
and leaving no forgiving trail
for those I will might never see again.

Praying to the lord for any soul to keep.

The Kings and Queens

I walked into a scene of disheveled
                        royalty.

Where sobbing from a lonely princess stained
a grieving carpet.

Self-imposed isolation will do that to you sometimes…
take you to places where the kings fall onto the bayonets
and the queens leisurely mention that
they wish death would happen quickly.

This is not a play or the story of the infamous anti-hero.

This was a crawl into sober obscurity—thousands that
take part on their wake-up calls to work…
and lie down when the clock turns ten.

I sometimes seek the princess who cries;
wonder if she needs
a shoulder to lean on…

If she believes in fate, tempts the time not taken
when we come
to terms that we will all die.

Never to rule…
The days that lie before us.

Or that one minute
when we head to
eternal sleep.

Briggs and the Shawshank Piano

The piano notes in Shawshank Redemption,
so daunting,
so final.

Briggs knew it—the fear of living.
Every step out into the world is a
claw to the stomach; a knife that churns
when you attempt to try to converse
with the *normal*.

This is no way to survive…
this failure to understand mankind.

The piano still echoes—
Briggs carves his name onto a beam
in the halfway house.

The final act of a man who had enough.

The ivory keys…isolation.
Chords play…*listen*.

Think of your life story, one last time
in a span of seconds.

Then kick back the chair…let the neck break.

Over.

No more remorse, hatred or loneliness.

Listen…

Just listen…

Depression 208

My days are spent sleeping now—trying not
to remember my false self.

Although I lie in bed with self-guilt, still
consumed with my hatred for phoniness;

I realize that to survive,
I must be fake…

Convert work into money—
money into food—but I deserve
the right to be angry at the process.

For now, however, I've shut it down.

Far away from the salesmen and status grabbers who
walk with robotic skeletons,
who laugh at me when I cry alone, see me
as a problem to the status quo.

And as the morning hustle and bustle of
slobs and seekers scurry to seek the almighty nickel…
I am still infatuated by one thought:

There's got to be more than this.

Law Abiding Citizen

Breaking my laws over
the bridge of sea and sand is
punishable by jumping into
the lonely abyss.

My justice, however, is irreverent
when the tone of love letters, books
and the jotting of thoughts become passé.

Old…ancient—no jury to hear my case.

I am a relic, a believer in
abilities that do not have to be
broadcasted.

Being fair to your fellow man, listening
to John Lee Hooker with new thought and insight.

No, my kind does not exist anymore. They either
have left the tournament early—well into the first half
or leaped into a fog of mysterious uncertainty where only
the dead know the truth.

It is these questions that make me a sad jester.

Broken.

Busted and battered…like those who have crashed into the sea;
shattering their bodies and never coming back.

A fitting sleep for those whose wounds could never be healed.

They are found innocent in my courtroom…silver saints
who expressed themselves so well
                so quiet
                and so misunderstood.

New York Journal Entry

A light shuts off at
dawn in the Empire State Building.

Someone must be working and
dying in the Big Apple.

Again…

A Plea to Arthur Rimbaud

I cannot walk the steps
you did Arthur…shuffling through
broken seaports with questions
about life and leisure.

My drunken boat has
been shipwrecked for years,
weighed down with lost hope
and broken dreams.

We sometimes may see the same, visions
of beast and scum that troll beneath our feet.

But Arthur, what do I do to find
                        you?

Conceptualize this world in longing phrases?
Desire underground liaisons between unkempt
lovers, villains and fools?

Arthur…my punishment for being too
observant is isolation. I do not have
the desire to search the world and find that
one moment…that one situation,
that will lead me out of the banal and into a final truth.

Arthur…help me ship out the doldrums—
show yourself just once more before I arrive,

In a dead land, time and space.

Take me there Arthur…

Take me…

Gutter Mind

The blood on my lips does not
mean I'm a vampire.

I just spew out sick sardines
when the mood strikes me
to speak in fantasized tongues.

Saying very little—something about sickness
that inherits the earth.

But don't let that get you down, I've
slept with legal prostitutes in Worcester
and I can tell you brother…their night habits
aren't great either.

So, pick your bones clean witnessing the
vermin warfare, the grossest point of no escape.

Because when it can't go any lower—it always does.

The Coffee Shop Man

I kept looking at him through
the corner of my eye as he peered
intently into his coffee cup.

Occasionally, he would manage a
sad smile as the waitress tried to
make small talk.

But it was forced conversation, for
his grin was weary…

Defeated…

He continued to look down at
his coffee; eyes welling but not
enough to create tears.

Maybe he was a widower
or just old…knowing his
years are growing short.

Sir, my reflection on this earth
is your stare, often I look down
at my own hands…afraid to extend
myself to anybody.

My loss is your loss.
We do not have to discuss anything
or walk out together.

I can tell from being here on this day
that we share a sad kinship…

As we leave separately…

Never to meet again.

Willem

He has walked the same path to
the same supermarket for over
thirty years.

Willem once looked like a
young Nazi; hair slicked back,
nose in the air, haughty defiant strut...

Only the goose step was missing.

The 9th grade cool kids would
yell at him from the bus, *Hey
Hitler—the war is over,* which
would send him into a maniacal tirade.

*I will eliminate you all someday...I will
cut out the middle man.*

The teeny boppers would
laugh as they sped away...
leaving him to continue his stroll.

Yesterday, I saw Willem while
driving to my shrink appointment.

His hair much greyer, his stomach
much larger…his pace however
still the same.

I do not know if he is looking for the middle
man anymore…nor if he has the desire to
eliminate us all.

I do know that the Germans lost the war many years ago.

Willem is still searching…losing the battle.

As am I…

No More Lines

We walk within these lines
of faded obscurity…

The problem is I do not
know who the we are anymore.
Decapitated idealist whose teeth
are about to fall out due to age
and time that fails to return…

Physically have we lost the battle?

Knees crack, shoulders reek of pain
when movement occurs.

I notice that poetry still lives
among some who's strength conquers
old age but my oh my preambles and
sayings fail to even shoot out the porch light.

Are we back to us? Those whom climb the fence,
raring to head back into the insane asylum?

Me? I am now a babbling idiot…searching for the touch
of Golden Fleece to fight the obedience of being too old…

I am now a glorified court jester…my bald head
freezing in the wind…

Finding Your Kingdom

It's as simple as getting cut off
in traffic.

Another battle lost until you stop,
get out of the car,
find a snakeskin from the ground,

wave it in the air…

and proclaim yourself king…

At least you're a God of something

Now…

Kerouac's Fall Afternoon

Reading raw words by Ti Jean…the sorest of words.
Grey, cloudy New England Afternoon…

Fall…

when tears start raining death—
my soul is shredded into pure, utter sadness.

The late stages of life—falling… ending another day,
another game of nowhere journey.

Ti Jean…

Part of me hates you for being so true.

Looking for Johnny's Guitar String

She tried to find
John Lee Hooker's e-string in
the bowels of some dive in
heated New Orleans.

Her white, pale skin
burns
to a crisp; asking all the outdoor
barmaids if Johnny has been around lately.

She is obsessed with the search of
this one string, to finish her steps of happy.

She kicked the needle habit, kicked the hatred that
lived in every pore of her body.

Just this one pang of echo…to the *how-how-how*
of Mr. Hooker.

Alas, John died in 2001.

Nobody got around to telling her the news.

Upon hearing that her quest was over,
she slowly rolled up her sleeve and looked
at all the tire tracks that told stories of condemned
buildings and long nods into warm blanket oblivion.

The needle…oh the hot, phallic loving needle she
loved but hated so much…

Mr. Hooker—yes, he was gone,
probably to a much better place.
Soon so would she…buried in a hot-box…
somewhere in rural Louisiana.

Thoughts While Walking the Dog

If there cannot
be any truth to
the thoughts in
your head…

Must there be
lies to the steps
you take?

I am envious to the
recede of life, marginal
comments concerning
those who do not want
to participate.

The message is about
to be said—do you dare hear?

But the whole story
is never spoken until
one who is on the fringe
dies, then the sorrow,
the obligatory forget.

Even then—all our questions
shuffle on while the world moves
and rules our natural life.

Once a Blindness

To those who do not see,
who float in slow film frame
like a 1920's movie.

Your eyes are white
but with no pupils—surrounded
by 19th century books of
philosophers.

Seizing the sky with no glaze
but presence.

The lone player
of nuclear music around
the gallery.

It is foreshadowing of
once a blindness—that dances
in the terror of the wistful night.

The heroine stares up
into the catastrophe once
she falls from earth.

Past the sounds of gentle
words spoken by surreal poets.

She cannot perceive, but feels the
death around her…but she also cannot die.

The lady covets her soul.

Without name.
Without vision.

Jeff's Walk

Some asshole said once
the lonely will suffer.

Jeff thinks about this quote
as he adjusts the collar
on his coat.

Ready to walk
down the driveway,
then turn left toward
the empty woods—full
of dead sounds and screams
from the echoes of nothing.

He slips and falls,
skinning his knee on the icy road,
when suddenly he screams the line
that he was pondering five
minutes ago.

*THE LONELY
WILL SUFFER.*

No one is around
to hear him.

Fewer are present
to care.

Writer's Block

I blew off the shrink appointment,
didn't take my lorazepam
or spill confessions to my mother...

I am just sitting, beer on the table,

typing these words in Times New Roman...

trying to find my voice,

and failing.

The poems have come up empty...
not that my heart hasn't been in it—or from
a lack of trying,

but,

I just can't get the right combination down to
express the anger, the hatred, the disillusionment I
have for my surroundings...

Maybe I should just say it straight out...

And be condemned to another day of fighting it
out with the spirit.

Maybe my poet friends are saying…It's another
Provost poem about being unhappy.

Maybe my family will read this crap and worry
about my depression.

Maybe I won't care and post this fucker on Facebook…
Let all those who criticize hide in the corner; not having
the balls to say anything to my face.

So many great ones today still laying the blood
on the page…

But I'm still here…sleeping low, fighting off stuff
that would kill a large animal.

Tears still stream, isolation is my way of living…

And I still can't lay the lines on the fucking page…

Tyson and Cobain

Mike Tyson never believed that Cobain
could ride a moon beam.
He was just another brawler, ready to reap the rewards
of beating people up.

The intellectual stuff was for the computer geeks and
butterfly collectors Tyson must have thought.

As old Kurt flew to places only a young Pound
could fathom.

Mike wanted instant gratification; a wife to hit,
a bar patron to punch—while Kurt craved cerebral…
wanting to see the world with visceral eyes…
brooding about the search.

Blinded colors, frightened children…afraid to live in the
transcendent world of mind speak.

Tyson now has a tattoo on his face;
strained to be remembered as a great fighter.

Cobain is dead…he's buried somewhere in Seattle
with a shotgun hole in his skull.

I wonder if Mikey still thinks of Cobain…
and the strange way each pursued nirvana…

Do You Care

Never
Never
Never have I claimed I
was born of innocence…
Only the scars that claim
to be crow's feet appear to
be remains of all night vigils.
Words are typed with a plan
of escape, the webs they weave
leave the reader to places
well worn…tightened in the gut
by experience.
Self-evaluations portrayed to
the singers, laughers and fools
to be swallowed, cut up and depowered
by the very few…
who give a damn.

Imagery

Imagery is never clean, only a naïve fool whose daily
anticipation is attending a Boy Scout meeting can see
the world as clear and chaste.

A borderline glare into infinite dirt is an episode
for the theater of disdain.

Malingering loners who never know if tomorrow will come,
evil creepers who base morality on stolen merchandise.

Trees breezing in the wind, gardens full of flowers are not
options to those who live on the other side of the hill.

Imagery is filthy, bare…sullen to longing victims of want.

Those who beg for stability,
but only achieve a livelihood through violence and death…

Notions of peaceful delight…refuse to exist…

For them…

Kids in Florida

The Trials of Nuremberg
never slowed down the anguish
that man tried to pass on within a stepping stone
of dissociated guilt…
And if Buddha is your *thing*
well then bow down to the chanting
harmony of want…

Do we ever climb into the space that
saves seventeen kids? Theorize what
agony is within our own little mind…

Prancing with false bravado…
a Twitter rant or faceboob comment about
how actors can play the role of deviant
political farce…
Then the sickening larva will
lick their glistening lips…looking
over the bodies of souls in camps or
step around the blood of a freshman band member…

Crying *the horror, the horror*… That was good
enough for Marlon Brando…but it could never
extinguish the rationalization of another, another
pathetic look-away.

Depression #122

Ransacked
by lives so called
accountability,

I decided to
run out in the
rain and disturb
my neighbors in
the middle of the day.

Just to let everyone
know I wasn't working
and playing my role in
a reclusive society.

My depression and anxiety
have hit morbid levels—leaving
questions of tolerance of meds,
questions of existence sacred secrets
and more questions of where I'll be
tomorrow at 12:45 PM.

Unlike the Ancient Mariner, I
cannot find a break in the storm
to pray…The Albatross hangs around
my neck like Flavor Flav's clock.

Time is not going to unlock this penance
only slow baldness of soul…

That lives around the corner, the block and the state of
the world.

Smoking Character

I get stoned in front of words…
Typing furiously, getting at nothing
but excuses…falsely identifying
empathy for just cause…turn
down the heat just to live
and repeat again…

A thought goes away…leaving
nothing but writers block…
back to the pipe and an imagination
full of failure…

Currently based in Dallas, **Paul Koniecki**'s latest books of poems are, *After Working Hours* from NightBallet Press, *Reject Convention* by KleftJaw Press, and *Tom Farris is my Safe-Word* from CWP Collective Press. He was once chosen for the John Ashbery Home School Poetry Residency, met John Dorsey in a burlesque-house in Milwaukee, and read at both of the legendary Kansas City Throwdown Poetry events. He is the co-founder and co-host of *Meet Me With Curiosity* Poetry In The Park at Klyde Warren Park in Dallas, Texas. He married the poet Reverie Evolving in a bookstore and dreams about cashews.

Nadia Wolnisty is a poet, artist, and performer in Dallas, Texas. Her work has appeared in *MadSwirl.Com, Apogee, Philosophical Idiot, Spry, McNeese Review, Essay Daily, Paper & Ink*, and the *Art Uprising* anthology "Desolate Country," among others. She has two chapbooks: *Manual* from Cringe-Worthy Poetry and *A Zoo* from Finishing Line Press. A chapbook is forthcoming from Dancing Girl Press.

Abigail Beaudelle, 26, lives in Independence, Missouri with her husband Jacob Johanson and a rotating cast of children, pets, and plants. She spends her days and nights dreaming. Abigail can be reached for comments, questions, or conversation at language.of.fruit.trees@gmail.com

Dan Provost's poetry has been published throughout the small press for a number a years. He is the author of nine books and live in Berlin, New Hampshire with his soon to be wife Laura Cleaves and their Bichon Frise Bella.

This project was made possible, in part, by generous support from the Osage Arts Community.

Osage Arts Community provides temporary time, space and support for the creation of new artistic works in a retreat format, serving creative people of all kinds — visual artists, composers, poets, fiction and nonfiction writers. Located on a 152-acre farm in an isolated rural mountainside setting in Central Missouri and bordered by ¾ of a mile of the Gasconade River, OAC provides residencies to those working alone, as well as welcoming collaborative teams, offering living space and workspace in a country environment to emerging and mid-career artists. For more information, visit us at www.osageac.org

www.ingramcontent.com/pod-product-compliance
Lightning Source LLC
Chambersburg PA
CBHW021006110526
R18275700001B/R182757PG44588CBX00008B/13